D0667540

When all is ready and a good kettle of water boiling,
prepare the table in the drawing room – this may or may
not be covered with a cloth according to its kind, but
if one is used it must be as dainty as possible – there is
nothing prettier than the all-white cloth,
embroidered or trimmed with lace.

Cold tea as a refreshing beverage is a capital sustainer.
One or two cups taken without milk or sugar are as
reviving and stimulating as the same quantity of sherry;
and a taste for this beverage is worth acquiring by those
who need an occasional and harmless restorative.

TEA

an

everyday

indulgence

ALSO CONTAINING
HOW TO ENJOY TEA:

ALSO CONTAINING
FRIENDS FOR TEA;
HOW TO CREATE
TEA TIME TREATS;

USES OF TEA LEAVES;
FRIENDSHIP AND REFLECTION;
WISDOM IN THE TEASPOONS;
TEA TIME TRIVIA;
AMUSEMENTS & GOOD TASTE.

Copper Beech Publishing

Published in Great Britain by
Copper Beech Publishing Ltd
This edition © Copper Beech Publishing Ltd 2007
Compiled by Jan Barnes
Additional contributions by Beryl Peters

ISBN
978 1 898617 43 3

A CIP catalogue record for this book is available from the
British Library.

Copper Beech Gift Books
Copper Beech Publishing Ltd
PO Box 159 East Grinstead
Sussex England RH19 4FS

Afternoon tea is one of the most sociable and popular events of the day. This very British institution is now enjoyed throughout the world. Whether you are alone with your cup, enjoying the company of friends, or planning a more formal gathering, tea is the perfect everyday indulgence.

THE MOST SOCIAL AND POPULAR EVENT

&

Refinement of the hostess

Afternoon tea is that light refreshment taken in the afternoon to break the fast between luncheon and late dinner. It is usually served in the drawing room between four and five o'clock and can be quite unceremonious in character.

The best that can be afforded
Tea is one of the most social and popular events of the day and the taste and refinement of the hostess are readily recognised in the manner in which it is served. Everything should be as dainty and attractive as possible. The tea itself should be of the best that can be afforded and must be well made.

HOW TO MAKE TEA

Good fresh tea

Half fill the teapot with boiling water, let it stand a minute or two until thoroughly hot, then empty it.

Put in the requisite quantity of tea (the old rule of a level teaspoon for each person and one over is a good one, but for a larger number of people, a smaller proportion may be allowed).

Pour on, gently enough, boiling water to half fill the teapot. Take the teapot to the kettle and never the kettle to the teapot.

Cover with a tea cosy and let it stand in a warm place to infuse for three minutes, then fill up the teapot and pour out the tea.

Tea is never good if allowed to stand too long, and the use of a tea cosy is to be deprecated if it is employed to keep tea hot for a long time.

If tea has to be kept hot for any length of time, it should be poured off the leaves into another teapot, or some teapots are fitted with an inner case which contains the leaves and which can be removed when the tea has infused sufficiently.

When sugar and milk or cream are used, they should be put into the teacup before the tea.

Take the teapot to the kettle and never the kettle to the teapot.

TEA PLANT.

Tea is a beverage which is said to comprise the active constituents of the most powerful mineral springs.

TEA AS A RESTORATIVE

A most excellent drink

Tea, taken in an infusion, has long been noted as one of the very best and most reliable restoratives. The leaf of the tea shrub being boiled and infused in water, is drunk as hot and as often as you please.

Exhilarate the spirit

Tea is said to have a diuretic faculty, to much fortify the stomach, exhilarate the spirits, and wonderfully open all the veins.

Improves concentration

Written reference to the tea leaf was first noted in the 3rd century BC when a Chinese surgeon recommended it for increasing concentration and alertness.

It is the done thing:

To have the day and hour of an afternoon tea
engraved on one's visiting-card, or written
if one prefer it so.

To give simple refreshments at an afternoon tea.
One need only provide tea, with thin slices of bread
and butter or sandwiches, fancy biscuits or cake.

To remember that a large afternoon tea and a
reception are very much alike, the latter being
usually more formal in character.

The *'At Home'* is usually omitted, the card for one
or more receptions containing, in addition to the
names of the hostess and her daughter, and their
address, the day 'at home', and the hour, using
letters instead of figures for date and hour.

It is not the done thing:

According to the newest fashion, to put the day of the month or the hour in figures in an engraved invitation.

To use the letters 'am' or 'pm' in an invitation, instead of 'o clock'.

To give champagne or wine at an afternoon tea.

To have the rooms over- or under-heated.

To give a handsome supper where the guests have been invited to afternoon tea.

To use a low five o'clock tea-table where a number of guests are expected, thus obliging the hostess to jump up constantly and sit down to pour out tea.

*Scones and teacakes are best hot buttered and served
in a muffin dish or in a folded doyley. Different kinds of
small sandwiches might also be served and there
must always be a nice choice of cakes.*

SMALL GATHERINGS

Little preparation is necessary

The smallest and most familiar form of afternoon tea is when a lady invites a few guests known to each other, or one or two of whom specially desire to make each other's acquaintance. Such invitations are issued verbally or by note, and little preparation is necessary.

A low table for a small gathering
The table is generally low and should be placed beside the hostess. The plates of cake may be placed on a cake stand or on another small table close at hand. Infuse the tea and fill up the hot water jug or kettle last of all and carry all to the drawing room at the hour appointed.

A MORE FORMAL AFFAIR

ॐ

… all kinds of dainties

At very large 'at homes' tea is frequently served in the dining room, but this is a more formal affair, and the food is more substantial.

When visitors arrive

Visitors are shown into the room on arrival. The table should be made into a sort of buffet. It must be covered with a fine damask cloth and the serving should be done from the back. Both tea and coffee are frequently served on these occasions and rows of cups and saucers should be in readiness.

Cream, milk and sugar

The jugs of cream and milk and bowls of sugar might be placed on the side of the table next to the guests, allowing them to help themselves.

An abundant supply of food

There should be an abundant supply of all kinds of dainties, and one or two large cakes on high stands would help to give an ornamental appearance.

The table must be prettily decorated with a few flowers or plants and everything made as attractive as possible.

The gloves are not usually removed when tea only is taken, but occasionally it is necessary to take them off.

FIVE O'CLOCK TEA

ﻉﻮ

Biscuits are invaluable

At small five o'clock teas, tea is handed round in the drawing-room, and it is unusual to employ a servant to hand the cups.

Gentlemen will naturally help

The hostess dispenses the tea herself, and if there are any gentlemen present they naturally undertake the task of giving each lady her cup of tea, handing her the bread and butter and cake, and taking her cup from her when empty. In the absence of gentlemen, any young girls who are friends of the hostess will volunteer to assist her.

The difficulty of gloves

If the bread and butter is carefully rolled so that none of the butter appears upon the exterior of the bread, it will be found possible to partake of it without removing the glove. This is frequently a task of so much difficulty that, rather than undertake it, the visitor often takes her tea without eating at all; a practice which the doctors consider to be very injurious to the digestive organs!

The thoughtful hostess

Biscuits are invaluable for this reason, and the thoughtful hostess will always provide them. Petits-fours and other fancy biscuits of various sorts are also favourites as they are dry and not likely to soil the gloves.

Sandwiches

The variety of little sandwiches is endless, and the following hints will prove useful. Sandwiches may be made of white or brown bread, or small rolls, filled with meat, salad, eggs, fish, or flavoured butter and made up in a variety of ways.

The sandwiches may be cut in various shapes, square, triangular, oblong or diamond. Very dainty little sandwiches can also be made by spreading a tasty mixture on the bread and then rolling it up.

Butter for sandwiches

The butter used for sandwiches must be very good. If hard, it should be creamed first until it is soft enough to use. The knife may be dipped in boiling water so as to make the butter seem less hard.

Very thin

The thickness and size of the sandwiches depends upon the purpose for which they are to be used. For afternoon tea they must be cut very thin, and nothing of a substantial nature must be offered, as it would take away the appetite for dinner which follows after.

OUT SHOPPING

Stopping for tea

Many women nowadays will delight in finding a little tea room, stopping for tea and meeting friends when out for the day shopping.

A tax on tea

Back in the 1780s the tax on tea was greatly reduced, and tea soon became Britain's most popular drink.

Tea replaced alcohol

Tea replaced the ale common in most houses as a daily refreshment and source of nourishment. Tea was drunk at home, and then tea rooms and tea gardens replaced the then closed-down coffee houses.

A place for women to meet

Women at last had a place outside the home to meet and drink tea, and all social classes could enjoy the tea room as well as the pleasure gardens which offered fresh air, tea drinking and entertainment.

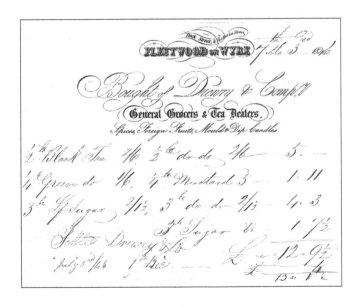

1846 bill for black tea, green tea and sugar

PAUSE FOR TEA IN THE 1880s

A fashionable event

The pause for tea became a fashionable social event.

Society women

During the 1880s, upper class and society women would change into long gowns, gloves and hats for their afternoon tea which was usually served between four and five o'clock.

TEA JACKETS IN THE 1880s

ॐ

these delightful materials

A tea jacket is always a joy. Moire velours, *crêpe de chine,* and old lace, put together as you will, must make a happy combination, but a tea jacket of these delightful materials manipulated by a master hand must be seen to be appreciated.

Smartness combined with comfort
There is no garment quite so delightful as a tea jacket, and when smartness is combined with comfort, nothing further can be desired, and any lady who is in want of such an addition to her wardrobe cannot do better than procure a pattern, and proceed to carry it out for herself without delay.

THE CERAMIC ART CO. Ltd., Cauldon Bridge, Hanley, Staffordshire Potteries.

Secrets of Success
Afternoon Tea Tableware

The beauty and delicacy of the china
is most important.

◄o►

It is usual to have small thin cups and saucers of
some dainty design with teaspoons of a suitable size.

◄o►

All the silver must be very bright.

◄o►

Plates are not as a rule required, unless cream cakes
or other similar dainties are being offered.

◄o►

When used, the plates must be quite small in size.

CHOICE OF CHINA

Avoid strong colouring

The choice of china is very much a matter of taste and circumstances. Before selecting, it is advisable to send for catalogues from some of the larger firms. Many valuable ideas may be gleaned in this way.

A style which can be replaced

The frugal housewife whose means are limited, and who will in all probability have to leave her china in the hands of inexperienced servants, will do well to buy the strong make of stoneware or semi-porcelain for everyday use and to choose a style which can be renewed when pieces are broken.

Patterns such as the willow, delft, rose bud, white fluted and white with a gilt or coloured band are always stocked. Strong colouring should always be avoided for tea.

A proper tea set

A small tea set will usually consist of the following pieces: twelve teacups, twelve saucers, twelve tea plates, two cake plates, one slop basin and one cream jug.

Metal teapots, when not used for some time, frequently
have an unpleasantly musty smell and give the tea made
in them a distinctly disagreeable taste. To prevent this,
place a lump of sugar in the teapot before putting it away.

A MATTER OF TASTE

It is safer to use a good blended tea

The question of what special tea to use is entirely a matter of taste.

An acquired taste

China tea is appreciated by many people and it is light and refreshing. However, it is a an acquired taste and not liked by everyone; so, when tea is to be served to a mixed company whose individual tastes are not known, it is safer to use a good blended tea with no pronounced flavour.

It is the done thing:

To have several varieties of delicate and pretty cakes,
and several kinds of sandwiches and bread and
butter, also salted almonds, or other dainty
trifles on the afternoon tea table.

To give oysters, salads, patés, boned turkey, ice cream,
bonbons in the dining-room or the drawing room.

Some hostesses now give a great variety of
sandwiches, either made into a roll, or flat, and filled
with lettuce or other salad, paté-de-fois-gras, cheese,
nuts of various kinds, jelly, marmalade, caviar, etc.
and bread and butter of different sorts.

It is now the fashion to omit more solid articles
of food at afternoon occasions.

It is not the done thing:

To allow the tea to stand on the leaves, since this renders it unwholesome. It should be made in an earthenware teapot, and transferred quickly to a silver one.

To have tea poured out in the drawing room when many persons are expected, because the arrangement would be an inconvenient one, and would crowd the guests.

For guests to deposit their cups or plates in the drawing room in a careless or awkward manner, setting them on varnished surfaces or on silken cloths, or too near the edge of a table, so that they will be likely to fall upon the floor.

PREPARATIONS AND PLANNING

ह≈

Fresh tea and more bread

When guests are expected the table is sometimes prepared beforehand, leaving only the tea and water to be carried in when it is required.

Have the maid ready to bring fresh supplies
If more visitors should arrive after the tea has been served, the maid must see that there is a sufficient number of cups and bring more if necessary without requiring to be told. Fresh tea should also be made and more bread cut if needed.

Tea is usually poured out by the hostess or by a grown-up daughter and the cups are passed by any gentlemen visitors or by the young people of the house. Servants do not as a rule remain in the room, but are only rung for when anything extra is required.

Most varieties of scones may be split, and the pieces toasted, buttered, and served hot for tea. These hot cakes are particularly welcome during the cold winter months.

Secrets of Success
Scones and Teacakes

The great secret of success in making teacakes and
scones is to cook them as quickly as possible after
moisture has been added to the mixture. If this
rule is strictly adhered to, they will be
light and appetising.

—◄o►—

Any variety of hot cake should be served on a hot
plate or dish, preferably with cover. Many people
place this over a bowl of hot water, as half-warm
buttered scones or cakes are not appetising.

—◄o►—

When buttering scones the butter should be
softened, so that it can be placed on them very
lightly. They should be split when necessary with
a heated knife.

Pancake scones

Required: One pound of flour

Quarter of an ounce of carbonate of soda

Half an ounce of cream of tartar

One egg

Three ounces of caster sugar

One ounce of lard

Milk or buttermilk.

Beat the sugar and lard together to a cream, and to this mix in the egg well beaten up. Then add alternately the flour and enough milk, or buttermilk, to mix the whole in a thick batter.

Take some extra lard, rub a little of it on the griddle, after first heating it, then pour a little batter in as neat rounds as possible on the gridle.

Cook the cakes from five to eight minutes, turning them once. Split open and serve very hot, with a liberal supply of butter.

Edinburgh scones

Required: One pound of flour

Three teaspoonfuls of baking powder

Quarter of a teaspoonful of salt

One ounce of butter

One ounce of caster sugar

One ounce of lard

One and a half ounces of currants

One egg

Half a pint of milk, or buttermilk.

Cake-Stand.

Mix together the flour, salt and baking powder, clean and add the currants. Beat up the egg, add the milk, then mix these gradually into the flour, etc., to form a rather wet dough. Turn it on to a floured board, and knead it lightly. Next roll it out until it is half an inch thick. Cut into neat triangular pieces, put them on a baking-sheet and bake in a moderate oven for about twenty minutes. These are excellent either hot or cold.

Half a teacup usually equals four ounces

THE IMPORTANT JOB OF
THE PARLOUR MAID

… see that the table is sufficiently supplied

The parlour maid would always have taken sole charge of the silver, glass, and china in daily use. She also had charge of the sideboard, the cake, fruit, etc and saw that fresh supplies were ordered as required.

Another duty

The care of the table linen would be another of her duties. She saw that the table was sufficiently supplied and that an accurate account was kept of the stock. Mending, too, might be done by her if time permitted.

If there is no lady's maid the parlour maid may be called
upon to wash and care for any fancy articles
such as doyleys and tray cloths.

TABLE LINEN

The dainty freshness

It has often been said that the refinement of a household may be judged by its table and more particularly by the dainty freshness of the table napery.

Nothing prettier than white

There is nothing prettier than the all-white cloth but if colour is introduced, it must tone with the colour of the teacups. Small serviettes to match are sometimes used, but this is not a universal custom.

The soiled and crumpled table cloth replete with holes is characteristic of the third-rate lodging house and not of the well-ordered household!

Small articles such as tray cloths, afternoon tea cloths, and doyleys are things frequently given as presents to those starting house for the first time.

"Tea had been brought into the drawing room and she turned her attention comfortably to the tier of delicacies on the cake stand. She chose a tempting morsel, poured out a cup of tea, and ate and drank ruminatively, her feet on the fender rail and her silk skirts 'hitched up' sufficiently to show a pair of Louis Seize shoes."

Secrets of Success
Small Talk

In nothing is the ease imparted by the habit of living in good society more apparent than in this very 'small talk' which is to true conversation as a game at 'beggar my neighbour' is to chess.

—<o>—

Be good-humoured without being familiar.

—<o>—

Be playful yet not loud.

—<o>—

Suit what you say to the person to whom it is addressed.

—<o>—

Those who have a gift of small talk get on a thousand times better in society than those who, lacking it, have better hearts and clearer heads. The accomplishment may, however, be cultivated.

Secrets of Success
Small Talk

Sometimes even perfectly well-bred persons feel a difficulty in providing the kind of talk that is necessary for bridging over odd moments in society.

◄o►

To be perfectly at ease with another requires that one shall first be perfectly at ease oneself. This can scarcely be the case with those who are feeling their way for the first time in society.

Polish tea trays with dry flour. First wash the tray well
with warm water in order to remove all grease, and
when quite dry, scatter the flour over it
and polish with a soft cloth.

THE USES OF TEA LEAVES

ॐ

Many people throw the used leaves away!

After the tea has once been drunk, many people throw the used leaves away, thinking that they are of no further good.

This is quite a mistaken idea, and they should always be squeezed out of the teapot, and put in a jar or basin until required.

It is, however, a mistake to keep them for longer than a day or two, as they can become mouldy, and are then of course useless.

Carpets

When sweeping a room, a few tea leaves should be scattered about the carpet; they absorb the dust, and render the task of sweeping much easier.

Decanters

Glass bottles and decanters when stained may have tea leaves put in them, boiling water poured over and be left for some hours; shake up the water well, and then pour away, and the stains will be found to have disappeared!

*Tea leaves may be soaked in a bucket of water for an hour
or two, the water then poured through a strainer, and used
for washing varnished woodwork of all kinds.*

Secrets of Success
Cakes

The heat of the oven is of great importance, especially for large cakes. If the heat be not tolerably fierce, the batter will not rise. If the oven is too quick, and there is any danger of the cake burning or catching, put a sheet of clean white paper over the top.

—◇—

To know when a cake is sufficiently baked, plunge a clean knife into the middle of it; draw it out, and if it looks in the least sticky, put the cake back, and close the oven door until the cake is done.

—◇—

Cakes should be kept in closed tin canisters or jars, and in a dry place.

SEED CAKE

This recipe for old-fashioned seed cakes was taken from a manuscript book dated 1831:

One pound of flour, two cups of sugar, one cup of butter, one cup of milk in which has been dissolved one teaspoonful of cooking-soda, one tablespoonful of cinnamon, and caraway seeds to taste. Rub your butter and sugar together, add the milk, then cinnamon, then flour, and last of all stir in a generous quantity of caraway seeds. If it is not stiff enough to roll out thin, a little more flour may be added after it is on the pastry-board.

These will be found delicious at five o'clock tea.

A NICE USEFUL CAKE

Beat four ounces of butter to a cream; wash, pick and dry six ounces of currants; whisk three eggs, blanch and chop two ounces of sweet almonds and cut a spoonful of candied peel into neat slices.

When all these are ready, mix the dry ingredients (four ounces sugar, sixteen ounces dried flour, two teaspoonfuls of baking powder) together, then add the butter, milk and eggs and beat well. Put the cake mix into a buttered tin and bake for no more than one and a half hours. This cake will be very good.

TEA WITH EGGS 1669

To near a pint of the infusion of tea, take two yolks of new-laid eggs, and beat them very well with as much fine sugar as is sufficient for this quantity of liquor. When they are very well incorporated, pour your tea upon the eggs and sugar, and stir them well together; so drink it hot.

This is when you are come home from attending business abroad, and are very hungry, and yet have not the convenience to eat, presently, a competent meal.

ADVICE FOR CAKE MAKING INGREDIENTS

Eggs
Should always be broken into a cup. Breaking the
eggs thus, the bad ones may be rejected without
spoiling the others.

—◄o►—

Sugar
Should be well pounded and sifted through
a fine sieve.

—◄o►—

Currants

Should be nicely washed and dried in a cloth. They
should then be laid on a dish before the fire to
become thoroughly dry. If added damp to other
ingredients, cakes will be liable to be heavy.

—◄o►—

Butter
Use only good butter. Warm before beating.

The games should take place after tea and last about an hour.

A CHILDREN'S TEA PARTY

ॐ

An irresistible source of enjoyment

A children's tea party requires careful organising. Tea should be served about half an hour after the time notified for the arrival of the little ones.

A feature of the tea menu

Plenty of bread and butter, cut cake and cakes of all kind should be provided. If the party is to be over very early and no other meal is given it is better to have tea later in the afternoon and to make jellies and creams a feature of the tea menu, not omitting bonbons, which should always be provided at parties for the little ones, as they invariably prove an irresistible source of enjoyment.

CHILDREN'S TEA PARTY GAMES

ह≫

The best games

The parlour games described here are suitable for a children's tea party.

Musical Chairs

This is a very favourite game for children. It can be the means of turning a dull party into an extremely merry one. A row of chairs is arranged down the middle of the room, alternate chairs facing different ways. The chairs must be one less in number than the number of children playing. As soon as the music starts, the players must dance round and round the chairs and directly the music ceases each player must seat themselves. The fun begins with the scrimmage to obtain a seat as soon as the music stops. The player who is left with no chair is taken out together with one chair. This continues until there is a winner.

Consequences

Give each player a pencil and a piece of paper. Players are told to write down an adjective that can be applied to a gentleman and then fold the paper to hide what they have written. Each player then hands her paper to the neighbour on the left. *Consequences usually run in the following order:*

> An adjective applicable to a man.
> A man's name.
> An adjective descriptive of a woman.
> A woman's name.
> Say where they met.
> Say what he said to her.
> Say what she said to him.
> Say what he gave her.
> Say what she did with it.
> Say what she gave him.
> Say what he did with it.
> Say what the consequences were.
> Say what the world said.

The papers are then opened and read aloud.

Secrets of Success
The Picnic Spot

England is replete with beautiful little country places abounding in romantic scenery.

◂◦▸

Very often some historical ruin is the centre of a good rural picnic spot; in the case of an excursion to one of these the picnic would therefore be instructive as well as amusing.

◂◦▸

Riverside places present the additional attractive prospect of a pleasant row to vary the programme of the day.

… beautiful little country places …

A WELL ORGANISED PICNIC TEA

ॐ

… the most enjoyable

Of the many entertainments peculiar to the summer season, a well organised picnic tea is perhaps the most enjoyable. For a picnic tea to be a complete success, it is necessary that it should be well organised at the outset and that no detail should be overlooked.

Train or tram

A great deal depends upon the selection of a suitable spot. When one lives in the country, the opportunities for picnics are of course unlimited, but near every town there are rural spots easily reached by train or tram at small expense.

For a small party, a picnic is a comparatively simple matter, one or two tea baskets equipped with the necessary table requisites such as cups and saucers, spoons, forks, knives, plates, methylated spirits lamp upon which to boil the water, a kettle which usually consists of a teapot and kettle combined, tins for the biscuits, cakes, bread and butter, salt etc, will hold these and all the other necessary provisions.

THE NEW MIDGET TEA BASKET

Nothing as a rule is forgotten in a properly equipped tea basket and the tins are usually labelled in accordance with the goods they are to contain, so there is no chance of anything being overlooked.

QUICK AND EASY TARTLETS FOR A PICNIC

Flaky pastry can be used for the jam or fruit tarts or tartlets so suitable for a picnic tea.

When making up tartlets, the cases should be baked with a crust of bread to the required size put in place of the filling to keep the case the right shape, the filling being added after the pastry is taken from the oven.

For picnics in summer, a dozen or more pastry cases packed on top of each other like saucers take up practically no room and can be filled on the spot if a small pot of jam be included in the picnic hamper.

STRAWBERRIES IN SUMMER

In summer it is very usual to offer fruit. Strawberries especially add colour and a distinctive delicious flavour. These are best served in small quantities on little plates.

Glass dishes for serving fruit

Table glass should always be of as good a quality as possible and the design should be characterised by its refined simplicity. Too much design and ornamentation is a mistake as it tends to rob the glass of that bright transparency which forms the great charm of its appearance.

Very thin glass is no doubt appreciated by those who like dainty articles, but it requires the utmost care in the washing and drying.

GROW YOUR OWN

৪়

Strawberry crops require very little labour

If you are looking for something special to offer your afternoon tea guests, consider growing your own strawberries.

Strawberries will do extremely well on heavy clay soil, holding out and bearing through a long drought in summer. Strawberry crops require very little labour.

Put some plants in an early border facing south, the plants being 18 inches apart each way. This may seem a waste of room but if plants are too close together the fruit rots in a wet season. Hoe ground between plants; it keeps down weeds and slugs.

In April or May mulch the ground well. In June, (the best month for strawberries) pick your crop, wipe with a damp cloth and offer these delights on your finest cut glass dish.

STRAWBERRY PRESERVE

ॐ

Allow the sugar to warm by the fire

Allow the proportions in weight as follows.

Three quarters preserving sugar to one of strawberries, so if you have three quarters of a pound of sugar you take one pound of strawberries.

Always choose small or medium-sized strawberries, removing the husks and any decaying fruits before weighing. While you are doing this allow the sugar to warm by the fire. Take a preserving pan and add the bright red strawberries together with the sugar. Heat gently until the sugar is completely melted, then boil rapidly until set. If you add the juice of one lemon before boiling, this greatly increases the chance of a 'good set'.

Always leave strawberry preserve to cool before bottling.

CRUMPETS

a tea time treat

There is no better sight than a toasting fork holding a crumpet which is being gently toasted in the fire. The very thought of adding best butter to this dainty treat is almost unbearable!

Required: One pint warm milk

One pound flour

One ounce yeast

One large egg

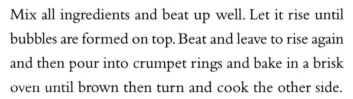

Half teaspoon sugar

A little salt.

Mix all ingredients and beat up well. Let it rise until bubbles are formed on top. Beat and leave to rise again and then pour into crumpet rings and bake in a brisk oven until brown then turn and cook the other side.

Crumpets are best served hot, toasted and well buttered.

It is absolutely correct to serve iced tea in summer,
flavoured with lemon.

GARDEN TEA PARTIES

ॐ

... a refreshing change

May, June and July are the months chosen for afternoon tea parties in the garden. Invitations are conveyed by cards similar to those used for evening receptions: *'Mrs. J. at home'* with the names of the invitees written at the top, and *'Tuesday May tenth four to seven'*, below.

It is courteous

It is unnecessary to answer one of these cards unless it is certain that the invitation cannot be accepted, when it is courteous to intimate the fact. Although the hour named is from four to seven, it is very seldom that any one appears before half-past four.

Iced tea

You may decide to offer iced tea and this would make a refreshing change.

The lady's maid

Tea, coffee and ices, are at the end of the table, generally presided over by the lady's maid. Waiters are engaged for the other portion of the table, where there are sandwiches, rolls filled with lobster salad, cakes, buns, fruit, claret and champagne-cup.

Entertainment

Sometimes these afternoon entertainments are diversified by amateur music, the grand piano being generally placed in the centre of the back drawing-room. Of course when there are professional singers the entertainment assumes the importance of a concert, chairs are placed in rows on the lawn. As for an evening concert, *'music'* is put in the corner of the cards, and programmes are provided, and distributed by the servants.

Cards for *al fresco* tea parties should bear 'Weather permitting.'

The next day

After an afternoon party, as after any other, cards should be left the next day, or as soon after as is possible, and whether the party has been attended or not. If at the last moment it is found impossible to attend, it is courteous to leave a note:

"Mr. And Mrs. P. and the Misses P. regret that they were unavoidably prevented having the pleasure of waiting on Mrs. B."

Ladies retain their hats or bonnets, inconvenient as the custom is very often found. A very large hat will be found very much in the way, and the smaller and lighter the headgear, the better for one's companion and for oneself.

A shady hat and one that fits well to the head is a real boon in hot weather. This pretty shape of Leghorn is bound with striped silk ribbon and trimmed with a fly-away bow.

It is the done thing:

To have the tea poured out in the butler's pantry if more convenient and to have it passed around by a servant, although it is 'better form' to have it poured out by the hostess or her deputy.

To be sure that the simple refreshments are the very best of their kind, using tea of superior quality accompanied by cream, cut white sugar and slices of lemon for those who like tea made in Russian fashion; also bread cut very thin and spread very daintily, with the crusts trimmed off.

To have the tea and coffee kept hot by means of urns with alcohol lamps beneath them.

To remember that cheap English breakfast tea is not fit to drink; while cheap Oolong tea is very good.

It is not the done thing:

To use powdered or granulated sugar for the tea and coffee, or lump sugar with chocolate.

To use cheap baker's, or poor or stale home-made cake.

To prepare iced tea in such a way that it has a bitter taste.

To have the tea cold or lukewarm.

To have the tea 'boiled' as this ruins its flavour.

To use tea of an inferior quality.

To make the tea with water which is not absolutely boiling at the moment when it is poured upon the tea leaves.

Secrets of Success
Pastry

The first secret of success in pastry making lies in keeping the ingredients and utensils as cold as possible and conducting one's operations in the coolest possible place.

—◦—

A marble slab may be employed with great advantage to roll the pastry out on in place of the more usual wooden pastry board.

—◦—

The hands should be held under the cold water tap for several moments and quickly dried before rubbing the butter into the flour when making a short crust.

Secrets of Success
Pastry

A knife should be used in place of the hands, whenever possible, and when kneading the dough preparatory to rolling it out, the knuckles should be used, these being the coolest part of the hands.

◄o►

Always let pies or tarts which are to be eaten cold, cool down gradually in a warm place after being taken from the oven Never put them into a cold place – such as the larder – until they are quite cold or they will certainly be heavy.

HOW TO MAKE PASTRY

෪

a light hand

Making pastry is a most useful accomplishment during the fruit season and a light hand for pastry is an art which every woman can very easily acquire.

Tartlets or pastry cases must be taken out of the tins and placed on a sieve in a warm place directly they are taken from the oven and allowed to cool gradually. If they are to be served hot, fill the cases with *hot* fruit or jam, never with cold, or they will be as heavy as lead!

Master these first

There are four varieties of pastry in common use: short crust, flaky crust, puff pastry and rough puff pastry. Short crust and flaky pastry are the varieties which are in everyday use in every household and these should be thoroughly mastered first of all.

THE HALLMARK OF A GOOD
SHORT CRUST PASTRY

The hallmark of good pastry is that it should be light, as full of air bubbles as possible, and to attain this end the flour must be sieved two or three times before being poured into the mixing bowl to aerate it thoroughly and the hands must be lifted high above the basin.

A feathery lightness

The flour and butter should be rubbed together with the tips of the fingers and scattered back through the fingers into the bowl from a height. This will allow each particle to retain a number of tiny air bubbles which, adhering to it, serve to isolate it from its neighbours, with the result that when baked the pastry will be beautifully crisp and of a feathery lightness.

This result can be attained in no other way.

Required: A mixing bowl

Pastry board or marble slab

A rolling pin

A knife

A jug of water

A pastry brush

A flour dredger half filled with flour.

Weigh out the butter and flour carefully on to squares of white kitchen paper and place all the ingredients in readiness on a dish close at hand before beginning operations.

HOW TO MAKE A FRUIT TART USING
SHORT CRUST PASTRY

1. The sieved flour is placed in the mixing bowl with the butter and a pinch of salt.

2. Rub the butter into the flour with the tips of the fingers until the whole resembles fine breadcrumbs.

3. The ingredients are now welded together with a small quantity of water poured in a trickle at a time until the dough is of just the right consistency.

4. The hands must now be floured with the help of the dredger, and the dough kneaded with the knuckles.

5. Flour the board or marble slab and rolling pin. Dust the dough with flour on either side and place it on the board. Next roll it out into an oblong shape rather longer than the dish it is to cover with as few passes of the rolling pin as possible.

Keep the edges of the paste as even as possible.

The pastry is now ready for use and it can safely be left while preparing the filling for the tart.

Prepare the fruit

The fruit for the tart, rhubarb, apple or gooseberries, must be prepared with a silver knife. If apples are used they must be peeled, cored and cut into rather thin slices and piled up high in the dish with the egg cup inverted in the middle of it, and four or five cloves and a thin strip or two of lemon rind and several spoonfuls of demerara sugar added.

It is essential to have the oven of exactly the right heat, and to judge this, test it with a strip of white paper before putting in the pastry.

Prepare the tart for the oven as follows:

1. Lightly flour the slab of pastry and cut a long narrow strip from one side.

2. Dip the pastry brush in water, damp the flat edge of the pie dish and cover it with the strip of pastry.

3. Next, damp the strip of pastry and gently put the lid of pastry on the top of the pie, pressing it down well round the edges.

4. Run a sharp knife all round the dish to cut off the superfluous pastry.

5. Press the edges well all round with the thumb and then flick up a fancy border with the back of the knife.

6. Make a slit in the top of the tart with the point of the knife, to let out the steam, after having brushed it over with water and sifted some white caster sugar over it – which will melt and make a pretty glaze.

The tart is ready to be put in the oven.

Prepare the oven

When the oven turns paper a pale yellowish brown in less than five minutes, it is just right and the tart should be baked in it for about half an hour or a little longer. Turn it once or twice to be sure it does not burn, and remember too, on no account slam the oven door, or it may make the pastry heavy.

FLAKY PASTRY

In making flaky pastry, only one third of the butter is rubbed in, the remaining two thirds being put on the rolled out pastry in little dabs and merely folded in.

1. Divide the butter into three equal parts. Put the flour and one part of the butter and a pinch of salt into a basin and rub the butter into the flour.

2. Mix into a stiff paste with a little water and roll it out into a long oblong strip, keeping the edges as straight as possible.

3. Dab the second portion of butter in little lumps over two thirds of the length of the paste, and fold it in three in such a way that the unbuttered piece of paste is between the other two.

4. Turn the paste with the folded edge to the left, flour and roll it out twice, folding and turning it to the left as before, but without adding more butter.

5. Now flour it and put it aside to cool between two plates for ten minutes, bring it back and roll it out again. Daub the remaining portion of butter over two thirds of its surface and fold and roll out twice as before, remembering to flour it between each rolling.

6. Put it aside again for ten minutes and it may then be rolled out in order to use it for a pie, tart or for making small pastry cases.

If bubbles are formed while rolling the paste, on no account try to roll them out or disperse them as they are a splendid sign that the pastry will be light!

*The first thing which every would-be pastry maker aspires
to do is to be able to make a good fruit tart, and for this,
either a short crust or a flaky paste may be employed.*

It is the done thing:

For the hostess, at a large occasion, to have the
assistance of other ladies in receiving her friends.
These assistant hostesses should move about the
rooms, entertaining the guests, asking them to go in
and take some refreshment, and making the
necessary introductions.

For the ladies who receive to wear a handsome
demi-toilette – made of silk, satin, velvet, lace or
some pretty woollen material, cut down at the neck
if the wearer chooses, and light or dark in colour.

It is now thought better style to wear a high-necked
gown. Young girls when receiving wear white or
light-coloured dresses of chiffon or some pretty thin
material, made high in the neck, with long sleeves.

It is not the done thing:

For the hostess to be stiff and formal in her greetings to her guests. An afternoon tea is an *informal* occasion.

For the hostess at a large reception to receive her friends without the assistance of some other person who can share the burden of hospitality with her.

To invite guests to meet some distinguished person, and then neglect to introduce them to him or her.

To introduce such a multitude of persons to a distinguished guest that your guest becomes wearied and confused.

For the hostess to wear full evening-dress.

THE TEASPOON

an uncertain quantity

As a medicinal measure the teaspoonful used to be only an uncertain quantity, as the teaspoon has varied so much in the size of the bowl.

Indulgence

Throughout the 18th century, when tea first became known to the working population, the tea-drinkers were almost exclusively women; men, even in educated classes, very often persisting in treating such a beverage as an idle and effeminate indulgence.

The female mouth

It was this twist in masculine habits that secretly controlled the manufacture of teaspoons. Up to the time of Waterloo, teaspoons were adjusted chiefly to the calibre of female mouths.

A FRIEND FOR TEA

ࣴ

… as agreeable as you can

When you have invited a friend to take tea with you, endeavour to render her visit as agreeable as you can; and try by all means to make her comfortable. Your guest should first be conducted to an unoccupied apartment as soon as she arrives, where she may take off her bonnet and arrange her hair.

Two tier table

For these friendly gatherings two tier tables are convenient; the upper shelf being occupied by the cups, teapot, milk, etc., the lower by the bread and butter, cake, and spare cups.

Close bonds

This is a special time when close bonds are cultivated and there is time for shared wisdom and reflection.

WISDOM IN THE TEA SPOONS

friendship

Even the most pretty and most confident of all your friends can sometimes need your friendly advice.

Over the steaming cups

Meeting over the steaming teacups is a good opportunity to help her to discuss her woes. When there are just the two of you together with your favourite brew, assure her that her confidences are safe with you and that you will proffer any assistance you can.

A friend in the future

After a couple of hours of friendly chat, you will know that you have someone to turn to should you ever need the hand of friendship in the future.

Friendship over the steaming cups.

If you are engaged to take tea with an intimate friend, and you afterwards receive an invitation to join a party to a place of amusement, which you have long been desirous of visiting, you may retract your first engagement, provided you send an apology in due time, telling the exact truth, and telling it in polite terms.

TEA PLANT.

Only the beverage made with the leaves of Camellia Sinensis should be called tea. Other brews are usually called herbal infusions or tisanes.

AFTERNOON TEA AND WHIST PARTIES

Friends agree to meet

Another form of afternoon entertainment, common only in the winter time, is the afternoon whist party.

Certain friends agree to meet on a certain day in the week for the purpose of the game, and the hostess is 'not at home' to any one not included in the coterie.

Bridge tea

If this is successful then consider planning a 'Bridge Tea' for which everyone would arrive promptly at 3.30 to drink tea and play bridge. Tea, coffee, and sometimes sherry are the refreshments usually provided at these parties, which are becoming yearly more fashionable.

A Winter's Afternoon

A cat and a dog, and a nook,
By a fire and a readable book,
A chum who drops in for a chat,
And to show her new 'duck of a hat'.

A kettle that's singing,
And someone who's bringing
Tea-cups on a tray.
Oh, the gloomiest day
With jollity, gladness is ringing!

The fire is poked into a glow
For muffins and crumpets, you know.
Some gossip and news
(Just to ward off the 'blues' -
For look! It's beginning to snow.)

A Winter's Afternoon

'Rat-tat'. It's a letter!
Some violets by post.
Some honey from home,
Which they pile on the toast!

They're cheery these four,
In the little town flat –
The girl, her chum,
and the dog and the cat!

Ian Drag 1927

It is the done thing:

For the hostess to move about the rooms, at a small or informal occasion, conversing with her guests and attending to their wants.

For ladies who are guests to wear plain tailor-made costumes, or handsome reception-dresses if they prefer, retaining their hats, but taking off their outer wraps or leaving them on, at will. White or light gloves complete the visitor's costume.

To provide a dressing-room for the ladies and for gentlemen also, when they are invited.

To remain at an afternoon reception half an hour or longer, if one should choose to do so, and find friends with whom to converse.

It is not the done thing:

To detain the hostess in conversation in such a way as to prevent her from attending to other guests.

For gentlemen to come into the drawing-room carrying their umbrellas with them.

Young ladies who are asked to assist in receiving or in waiting on the guests should not wear dark street costume. They may, however, wear silk waists and dark skirts on informal occasions.

To go to a lady's house to a tea when one has not been invited.

To go to *every one* of a series of receptions for which one has received cards. Thus if Mrs. Middleton sent out cards for 'Fridays in January' the same persons would *not* attend more than one or two of these.

A VERY CHARMING TEA COSY

ु॰

… to be washed as often as need be

A great objection to tea cosies is that they soon get soiled and there is considerable difficulty in cleaning them. People who use them are often less particular about their spotless cleanliness than they would be about that of the napery on the table.

Embroidery

Some people try to meet the difficulty by covering the embroidered surface of the cosy with a muslin slip cover, which can be washed as often as needful; but this muslin cover is so evidently a sort of pinafore that it is by no means to be recommended.

A sensible cosy

A very charming tea cosy is suggested here. The advantages of the cosy are that the embroidery of the outside and the lining of the cosy are all made to slip off and to be washed as often as need be, and merely have to be tied on again with some narrow ribbon strings for the whole cosy to look as good as new once more.

If you wish to make one of these very sensible cosies, look well at the diagrams, and then set to work in full confidence that your efforts will be crowned with success.

Fig. 1 represents the cosy itself. It is one of sateen, nicely padded, and is ornamented with silk all round the edge. The rest is hidden by the embroidered linen slip which forms the cover and lining.

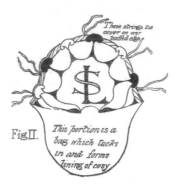

Fig. 2 shows how this cover is made, with the embroidered slip just ready to put on the cosy, with its ribbons dangling and the lining still hanging loose. This slip is formed of two pieces of white linen made into a sort of bag, the lower plain portion which forms the lining, and the upper or flap part. This is embroidered in linen thread or washing silk, and tied by means of ribbon passed through eyelet holes on the edge, to cover the whole of the outside of the cosy except the puff of silk. You can see the shape from the drawing, and see that the only seam is that which goes round the part which forms the lining.

Fig. 3 shows the cosy complete, with its lining tucked into place and the bows tied across the puff of amber silk.

Artistic designs are easy to find, and even if you cannot originate them, you will be able to understand how to make this cleverly contrived slip cover, for with a couple of these, and an occasional new puff of silk, a cosy might be kept fresh and new-looking for years.

ICED TEA

ह❧

A heat wave

In 1904 the United States was ready for the world to see her development at the St. Louis World's Fair. Trade exhibitors from around the world brought their products to America's first St. Louis World's Fair.

One merchant was Richard Blechynden, and he owned a tea plantation. He had planned to give away free samples of hot tea to the visitors at the fair, then a heat wave hit, and no one was interested in hot tea.

So that he did not waste the tea, this merchant added ice into the brewed tea and served the first 'iced tea'. It was a great success.

GENERAL DIRECTIONS FOR WASHING UP

ॐ

A plentiful supply of hot water

Before the washing up is commenced, a certain amount of preliminary arrangement is necessary. The most important is to see that there is a plentiful supply of hot water.

Remove scraps and crumbs

Next, everything that requires washing must be collected together and put within easy reach. All scraps of crumbs or jam must be removed from the plates; slops must be poured out of teacups; remains of tea and tea leaves from the teapot.

If this clearing is not done before starting the washing, the water would not only become necessarily dirty and require more frequent changing, but the work itself would be disagreeable.

Sort

Arrange all articles of one kind together, plates in neat piles, saucers in another pile, cups by themselves, etc.

Basins

Two basins are required, one for the washing in hot water, the other for rinsing in tepid water.

Fine china

For silver glass and fine china, a small wooden tub is less liable to scratch and break these fine articles.

Everyday tea dishes

If tea dishes are in daily use, it is sufficient to wash them in hot water with a soft mop; rinse in tepid water. Avoid excessive rubbing on finely painted china.

If water is too hot for the hands to rest in,
it is too hot for the china.

TISANES

Other brews …

Other hot brews, not strictly 'teas' now go under the name of 'tisanes' or herb teas. These drinks are said to have a variety of medicinal properties.

Clove tea – a natural laxative
Boiling water, made spicy by a few cloves will do evacuant good in more ways than one.

Peppermint tea – improves digestion
Something as simple as mint leaves from the garden infused in hot water will help a faulty digestion.

Chamomile – calming
Chamomile is said to relax and calm.

Ginseng – invigorating
Ginseng is claimed to have powers to invigorate the body and to act as a remedy for impotence.

MISCELLANEOUS HINTS

Stains on cups

Tea stains may be removed from cups and teapots by rubbing them with a little common salt or a little soap on a cloth and then applying it to the mark.

Nothing of a clumsy nature

A hostess should try to study novelty and variety foodstuffs, and nothing of a large or clumsy nature must be seen.

If the tray is not silver

All the bread plates should be covered with pretty doyleys or lace-edged papers. The tea should be prepared in the pantry and if the tray is not of silver, cover it with a dainty white tray cloth then arrange the cups, saucers, slop basin and cream jug on it.

TEA TIME ENTERTAINMENT

ૐ

An afternoon tea quiz

A quiz is always a popular form of entertainment, so why not include this quiz at your next afternoon tea with friends?

A quiz

At the top of your finest card, write the words 'Afternoon Tea Quiz' and then copy the questions out in your most decorative handwriting. You will be able to use these cards again and again with different guests. Have each guest provided with a pencil and paper. This quiz will be both amusing and informative, and your guests will learn more about their favourite beverage as they play!

Remember a little prize

Have an inexpensive prize ready for the guest with the most correct answers. This will add to the fun.

Afternoon Tea Quiz

Question

Who is credited with inventing the
British institution of afternoon tea?

Answer

Anna, 7th Duchess of Bedford, in the early 19th century
who had a hungry sinking feeling between lunch and her
8 o'clock evening meal.

Question

In which country was Assam tea grown?

Answer

Northern India

Question

Whose slogan 'Direct from the Tea Gardens to the Tea
Pot' became famous?

Answer

Thomas Lipton, because he cut out the middle man by
having his own plantations in Ceylon.

Afternoon Tea Quiz

Question

What is a 'mote' spoon?

Answer

This was the forerunner of the modern tea strainer. It came in to use in the 1790s. It was a pierced-bowl spoon with a long spiky handle. It was used as a caddy spoon so that the tea dust would fall through the holes and only the good tea leaves went into the pot. The spiky handle could unblock the clogged up spout.

Question

The words 'tea caddy' started to be used at the end of the 18th century. Where does the word 'caddy' come from?

Answer

From the Malay word 'kati' denoting a measure of approximately one pound five ounces.

Afternoon Tea Quiz

Question

Which canal was opened making shipping of tea easier between Europe and Asia?

Answer

Suez – was opened in 1869

Question

What was New York called in the days when the Dutch had colonised it?

Answer

New Amsterdam

Question

What was the Golden Lyon in 1717?

Answer

A coffee house owned by Thomas Twining and dedicated to selling loose-leaf tea and to serving both men and women. Before this women were banned because of the bawdy jokes, smoke and alcohol.

Afternoon Tea Quiz

Question

Which well known household management expert gave
instructions for serving an 'at home tea'?

Answer

Mrs. Beeton

Question

Tea was rationed in England in 1940. What was the
ration each week?

Answer

The ration was two ounces per person per week. It was
thought of as being a real life-saver.

Question

Does a cup of tea or coffee contain the more caffeine?

Answer

Tea, but it is released more slowly than the caffeine
in coffee.

Afternoon Tea Quiz

Question

What did 'bite-and-stir' boxes hold?

Answer

Powdered sugar to stir in to tea and lump sugar to nibble and drink the tea through.

Question

Who said 'Bring me a cup of tea and the *Times*'?

Answer

Queen Victoria, on hearing of her accession to the throne in 1837.

Afternoon Tea Quiz

Question

How did the idea for tea bags develop?

Answer

Some say it was in France around 1900. Others say that Thomas Sullivan of New York used to send samples of tea to prospective customers in little silk bags. The first tea bags proper were made from fine cloth or gauze in the 1920s.

TEA TIME TRIVIALITIES

There are a total of over 3,000 teas from all over the world; white, black, green, Oolong, scented and compressed. Each category contains many different varieties.

◄o►

Fermentation of green leaves produced better tasting black tea and this was developed around AD 650.

◄o►

The larger the tea leaf the longer you should leave it to infuse.

◄o►

Tea bags contain tiny leaves so infusion is immediate.

TEA TIME TRIVIALITIES

Earl Grey, Lady Londonderry and other socialites had blends of tea named after them.

◄o►

Dr Johnson was a 'hardened and shameless tea drinker'. His kettle hardly had time to cool before he was asking for another brew!

◄o►

Many deemed tea to be the favoured drink of the intellectual. It was a refined stimulant.

◄o►

The scalloped shell which appears on so many tea spoons originates from the time oriental merchants placed a real scallop shell in the tea chests so customers could inspect it before making their decision to buy.

'Eat lightly in the evening.'
While at morning and noon there is bountifulness, do
not have much on the tea table but dishes and talk. The
most of the world's work ought to be finished by
six o'clock p.m. The children are home from school,
the wife is done mending or shopping, the merchant has
got through with dry goods or hardware.
Let the ring of the tea-bell be sharp and musical. Walk
into the room fragrant with Oolong of young Hyson.
Seat yourself at the tea-table wide enough apart to have
room to take out your pocket-handkerchief if you want
to laugh or cry at any story of the day.

Other Copper Beech Gift Books to collect:-

THE SERVANTLESS HOUSEHOLD
How to cope - some polite advice

APPEARANCES
How to keep them up on a limited income

DAINTY DISHES
for slender incomes

KITCHEN COSMETICS
Beauty from the pantry

HALVING THE HOUSEWORK
Valuable 'retro' style advice from the 1950s

THE LADY'S DRESSING ROOM
Open the door to beauty and relaxation secrets from
days gone by. How to get up, fresh, beautiful and in an
amiable frame of mind with all your wrinkles
smoothed over -
and other fragrant tips from a golden age!

HOW TO ENTERTAIN YOUR GUESTS
A 1911 collection of indoor games
A companion book to 'The Duties of Servants'

THE DUTIES OF SERVANTS
The routine of domestic service in 1890.
Reproduced for your enjoyment now.

THE LADY'S BOOK OF MANNERS
Instructions showing how to be a perfect lady.

SOCIAL SUCCESS
The modern girl's guide to confidence, poise,
manners and tact.
1930s etiquette for all occasions.

For your free catalogue containing these and other titles write to:

Copper Beech Publishing Ltd
P O Box 159 East Grinstead
Sussex England RH19 4FS

www.copperbeechpublishing.co.uk